Good Teaching

GOOD TEACHING

A Guide for Students

Richard A. Watson

Southern Illinois University Press
Carbondale and Edwardsville

Library of Congress Cataloging-in-Publication Data

Watson, Richard A., 1931–
    Good teaching : a guide for students / Richard A. Watson
        p.   cm.
    Includes bibliographical references (p.).
    1. College teaching—United States. 2. College teachers—United
States. 3. College student orientation—United States. I. Title.
LB2331.W345   1997
378.1'25—dc20   96-24600
ISBN 0-8093-2111-4 (pbk. : alk. paper)   CIP

The paper used in this publication meets the minimum requirements of
American National Standard for Information Sciences – Permanence of
Paper for Printed Library Materials, ANSI Z39.48-1984. ∞

Mr. Chips, he dead.

Contents

Preface

You can get a good education wherever you go to school—junior colleges, vocational schools and institutes of technology, state colleges and universities, and prestigious private colleges and universities. The teaching in every one of these varies from great to awful, but you can find good teaching in them all. To find it, you have to know that good teaching is not of first priority at many colleges. And it may not be exactly what you thought it was. I tell why and offer advice about how to get good teaching anywhere.

Good Teaching

Introduction

You are now a college student, it costs plenty, and you think you deserve good teaching. So do I, but it's not that simple. Many colleges, particularly those that are part of universities, are not at all what you might think. Your high school was primarily a teaching institution, but your college may be first of all a research institution. It is thus important for you to understand the overall college and university system so you can have a realistic perspective on your professors and on college as it really is.

Let's define our terms. The name of the game is learning. You want good teaching because you want to learn. That's why you are in college, to learn something. You are in college to learn a trade, to qualify for a profession.

I grant that you may just want to learn some things, and you're not thinking of preparing for a job. Fine, I was once like that. My parents, however, were thinking that it would be a good idea if I could get a job when I graduated. (You can imagine what they thought when I majored in philosophy. Well, that was all right. It prepared me to be a college professor. Did it prepare me to be a teacher? Read on.)

You want to pass courses with good grades, get your degree, and prepare for a career. Good teaching can help you reach these goals, but you have to recognize from the beginning that it isn't necessary. You can get good grades from bad teachers, receive a degree without learning anything, and prepare for a career by making the right contacts. Good teaching is not even necessary to learning, because you can learn from bad teachers and even on your own. Am I saying that good teaching is a *luxury*? Well, it isn't an intrinsic human right, that's for sure. But it's nice to have, for good teaching can help you toward your goals. So let's define teaching on the basis of its effect on your learning:

1. Bad teaching hinders your learning.
2. Minimally good teaching at least does not hinder your learning.
3. Good teaching helps you learn.
4. Excellent teaching enhances your ability to learn.
5. Great teaching changes your life.

When I think back over the more than fifty years I have been among teachers—my father was a teacher; five of his siblings were teachers; four of my mother's were, and a dozen cousins; my wife is a teacher; her mother was a teacher; I am a teacher; my brother, his wife, and my daughter are teachers; most of my friends are teachers—I can think of only two or three who were great. But I've known many excellent teachers, and many more good ones. I never had a bad teacher myself, but I've known a few. Truly bad teachers are as rare as great ones, and most so ranked are at least minimally good.

Now here is a hard fact that we have to get around somehow. Most of your professors are set in their ways, and there isn't much you can do to change them. More to a very serious point, it isn't your business to change them. You certainly can help your professors to be good teachers, but your main business is to get an education. You have to learn how to use the professors you've got.

It is not your business to change them because students are birds of passage. This is what professors and administrators say to justify ignoring student suggestions about improving the college curriculum or the way the institution is organized. Here today, gone tomorrow. "But it's four years!" you say? Sure, but professors are around as long as forty.

The fact is that you are going to be in college only four years and that is little enough time to get a worthwhile education. You can't afford to waste your time (tuition costs money) trying to reform the college. I don't say that you couldn't. Students made big changes in the colleges in the 1960s, some good (decrease of parentalism), some bad (lowering of grading standards). What I'm saying is that pragmatically speaking, you've pretty much got to put up with the college situation as you find it, not just because you're a bird of passage, but also because you are in college for the very specific purpose of getting an education, not for the purpose of reforming the college. I'm not saying that the college situation as you find it is good or bad. I say it is what it is. I'm going to tell you how to contend with it. If you want to reform it, I recommend that you work without any disruptions toward getting a position in college administration, and *then* see what you can do.

But I don't mean that you should be a grind. Your college is one of the most congenial social communities you'll ever be a part of. You want to enjoy it and have a good time. Furthermore, let no one ever belittle your desire to find a compatible life's companion among your fellow students. You're here for several reasons, and finding good—even lifelong—friends is certainly a very important one. But it would be nice to have some good teaching, too.

1

Teaching

Who will teach the teachers?

—after Juvenal

My father taught mathematics and history and was coach and superintendent of schools in small towns in Iowa for nearly fifty years. He was the bane of the Iowa primary and secondary teachers certification board. Every state in the union has such a board, which requires that those who wish to be primary or secondary schoolteachers take at least a year of education courses in college to earn a teaching certificate. My father, who had an M.A. in education so he could be superintendent, had great scorn for education professors, courses, departments, state boards, and certificates. To subvert the system, he sometimes hired someone who had majored, say, in history but did not have a teaching certificate. Such people could get temporary certificates on the promise that they would fulfill the requirements by going to summer school Some did, some didn't. My father enjoyed sparring about it with school inspectors.

"You're either a teacher or you aren't," he used to say. He thought he could tell just by talking with someone for a while. "You can't teach someone to teach," he would say. "That's like trying to teach a bull to give milk."

My father's world was populated by teachers, almost all of whom had gone to teachers colleges and so had taken courses in teaching. My world is one in which virtually no professor has had any training in teaching whatsoever. Having grown up in the one world and having long occupied the other, I think the old man was partially right. There are born teachers. Or at least there are people who grow up to be confident, articulate, relaxed, and knowledgeable, who like students and enjoy teaching. They are enthusiastic about the subject matter, and they put it across with some flair. They don't need formal teachers' training.

There are others who do need training. But most of your college professors have had no training in teaching, so you get them as is. Those of your professors who actually don't like teaching or who don't want to teach certainly don't sit around evenings boning up on technique. The fact is that most professors think they are perfectly good teachers, so they don't recognize it when they have problems. If they do happen to notice defects in their technique, they usually try to keep it to themselves.

Born teachers aside, how *do* college professors get to be good teachers without any training? They learn—consciously or unconsciously—by observing their own teachers. That's why it's probably too late for most established professors to change the way they teach very much. Consider: A college professor is someone who has gone to school for twenty to twenty-five years. During that time, he or she has had sixty or seventy teachers. I won't calculate how many hours each of your professors has spent in classes observing teachers, but in all that time, he or she surely has learned the difference between good and bad teaching and has noticed the best tricks of the trade. Add to that several years of practice as a graduate student teaching assistant and as an assistant professor. If all that has not resulted in our hero's learning how to teach, can there be much hope for change now?

Sure, all is not doom and gloom. For beginning college teachers, there is some hope. I once knew an assistant professor whose students were complaining, and so a senior professor (not me) observed a class to see what the problem was. It was pretty simple. The assistant professor was behaving like a master sergeant, not allowing students to argue, putting them down, and in general not being very friendly. The senior professor recommended that the assistant professor loosen up, treat the kids like human beings, and let them talk a bit. The assistant professor seemed to be surprised by this advice and promised to change. But will someone like this actually change and become a better teacher? Probably, if the problem is merely nervousness, as in this case it may have been. But if we have a born master sergeant on our hands, don't hope for much.

What would you do if you had such a professor? What some students did was talk to another professor about it, one they could talk to about such things. There will always be approachable professors (and they may not, in fact, be the best teachers). Do I recommend that you be a busybody in this way? My advice, on the whole, is that it isn't worth the emotional flap. It will stir you up and waste more of your time than you have to spare. How long is a semester, anyway? You know, it's the only life you've got, the only time you'll ever take this course. So concentrate on the subject matter; that's what the course is about. In fact, if you do talk to another professor, what I've just said is probably the advice you'll get. Even if the teacher is truly bad, if you need the course, grin and bear it.

College teaching is quite a strenuous activity. A professor must remain mentally alert and prepared to discuss the same subject for an hour or more, under constant observation of a group of students, a remarkable number of whom are sometimes paying close attention. The professor is supposed to keep the students from falling asleep and teach them something. How he or she does it is worth study.

When you first come into a new class, observe and analyze the professor's teaching technique. This will take only a couple of sessions, because professors don't have large repertoires of tricks. Figure out your professor's goals for the course. Then determine how your professor is trying to accomplish these goals. Two extremes are, at the one end, professors who include in their lectures everything they expect their students to learn and, at the other end, professors who natter in class but expect you to know everything in the assigned reading for the exams. If you can classify your professors, you can adjust to their requirements.

You have to do the adapting because there are many adequate ways of teaching, and not all your professors will teach in the same way. You'll like some of them and dislike others. The teachers won't change—at least not in midsemester—so you have to be flexible.

I'm not going to say much about different techniques. One question, however, needs serious consideration. Should teaching be entertaining? Do you demand that your professor entertain you?

Why on earth should a professor be entertaining? There is no necessity that good teaching be entertaining. If you want entertainment, you'll watch television, right? A certain entertainment value does enhance teaching, but it is easy to go over the line so that entertainment hinders learning. A lot of professors are ham actors, which generally doesn't harm anything. But I'd trust a bad actor more than a good actor as a teacher. The reason is that high-level entertainers often persuade people to believe really foolish things. If you are a little embarrassed or disgusted by your professor's antics, you are less likely to be taken in. Entertainment makes powerful propaganda. That's why Plato abolished poets from his utopian community. You can see what Plato was getting at when you notice that although he excluded lyrical music, he kept martial music. He wanted soldiers, not dreamers.

I'm trying to twist slightly your notion of good teaching. You may not like some teaching I would call good. For example, some students seem to think that it is really good teaching when a professor passes out outlines of lectures, writes main points on the board, and provides summaries and key sentences for everything in the course. Well, that's nice, but not always good. Teaching should not be indoctrination; it should not be the imprinting of a mold on a student. You want to learn, and learning requires thinking on your own. You learn when you develop the ability to listen to a somewhat rambling lecture and outline the main points on your own. Good teaching definitely does not involve making learning as easy to swallow as a milkshake. But before saying just what it is, let me talk a bit about what your professors are teaching.

2

Subject Matter

You argue that a man cannot inquire either about that
which he knows, or about that which he does not
know; for if he knows, he has no need to inquire; and if
not, he cannot; for he does not know the very subject
about which he is to inquire.

—Plato, *Meno*

After the first day of my freshmen year in high school, I
reported to my father that the Latin teacher he had hired was
awful and that I was going to take something else. As it turned
out, I took Latin. To make a long story short, the lesson I
learned that day from my father was: Don't get hung up on the
teacher.

"I thought you wanted to take Latin," my father said.

"I wanted to take Latin," I told him, "but not from this
teacher."

"You want to learn Latin?"

I nodded yes.

"Then you'll take the course," he said.

"But the teacher . . ."

My father was not famous for patience.

"Forget the goddamned teacher!" he shouted. "Take the
course."

Can I put that in gentler terms? What my father meant to
say is this: Never, *never* not take something just because you
don't like the teacher. He went on to inform me that I'd get
some doozies when I went to college, so I might as well get

used to bad teachers now. Anyway, it wasn't all that easy to find a Latin teacher for a very small high school in Iowa in the late 1940s.

After a while, I learned to appreciate the Latin teacher, who could not keep order, was old and half blind, and somewhat forgetful, but knew her Latin and taught it well to anyone who would pay attention. It would have been a terrible mistake to give up Latin just because the teacher turned me off. She had come out of retirement to take this job, and she really was hopeless in many ways, but by the end of the two years of her employment, some of us even became protective of her. Not much, but enough to keep classroom noise down so we could learn Latin.

So never not take something just because you don't like the teacher.

This rule is based on the assumption that you know what you want to learn. But you may not yet know what you are most interested in. The way to find out is to visit classes in different subjects and then take courses in those you like best. Yes, we all know that this advice is both obvious and not very helpful. But it's the standard thing you'll hear. Keep looking, you'll be told. And, of course, if you really can't find something you want to learn, you're wasting money, and you'll certainly be bored in class.

We can do better than that, but it's hard to take. This chapter is about subject matter, right? Most students' problem is not that they don't know what to major in, but that they have too many interests and can't decide among them. That is why you shop around. But I remember when I did that, I just found more things I'd never heard of to add to my list. My adviser then had me take aptitude tests. I scored high on outdoor and humanities interests. So my counselor advised me to major in landscape architecture. My brother-in-law is a landscape architect, and it is interesting, but all the tests did was make me realize that compromise is not the answer.

Here, by the way, is the basic piece of wisdom my brother-in-law taught me from landscape architecture: "All right, lady,

I can cut that tree limb off for you. But just remember one thing. I can't put it back on again once it's off."

I am building up to the frightening conclusion that you are going to have to cut off some limbs. I think it's frightening, and if you are serious about your interests, you're going to find it frightening, too. Focus firmly on this fact: You can't do everything. You probably can't do two or three things. It is probable that you're going to have your hands full doing just one thing. You have to decide what that thing is.

I began my teaching career at the University of Michigan. The most junior person in the department, naturally, was given the job—in all the wisdom of his experience—of counseling freshmen. Time and again, I met students whose scores were about even in mathematics and science on one side and in verbal skills and humanities on the other side. Many times students said something like this to me:

"I'd really like to be a chemist, because I love lab, and I'd like to be a scientist. But history fascinates me, too, and I'd love to work in archives and write history books."

"Umm," I'd say.

"What do I do?"

I'd had a similar problem myself. I have degrees in both philosophy and geology and for some years did work in both. But even at the tender age of thirty, I realized that it was not good advice to tell someone to do both. I knew that if I were to advance in philosophy, I had better drop my work in geology. So I would say:

"Choose one. You can't do both. I've tried, and I know it's extremely difficult to do two different things."

"But which one?" would come the plaintive cry.

And here comes the frightening answer.

"It doesn't make any difference which one. Choose one of them. Flip a coin, if you must. Just choose one of them, and stick to it."

"But I'll always wonder if I made the wrong choice."

"Of course you will. But in fact, not all your life. If you truly are as interested in the one as in the other, then either one is fine. And as you get more and more into the field you choose, as you become a chemist, say, rather than a historian, the choice will seem more and more right to you, because that is what you'll be, a chemist."

"But what if I'd decided to be a historian, instead?"

"Same thing. It doesn't make any difference. You'd be a historian, and just as happy."

"But I want to choose the right one, the best one."

"You're avoiding the point. The point is that *whichever one* you choose is the right one. There isn't a best one. Or, rather the best one is the one you choose. You'll be happy with whatever one you choose, if you stick to it and don't look back. But as long as you balance between them and fret about which one to do, which one to choose, you'll be unhappy, and you won't really be able to do either one."

"But what if I really make a mistake? What if I chose chemistry, and then about the time I graduate, I see that I don't really want to be a chemist?"

"It's the gamble you take. At least you'll have found out. If you take a mishmash of courses in several fields, you'll never really know what you want. Again, if you truly have equal interests in several fields, it doesn't make any difference which one you choose. But for god's sake CHOOSE ONE OF THEM!"

I have inherited some of my father's short patience genes.

It's the best advice—even more so now than in the 1960s when I was a freshman counselor. Back then tuition didn't require mortgaging the family farm. Today it does, so you should be quite serious about finding out what subject matter you're interested in. You should be in college for a purpose, such as preparing for a career. Most students should settle down to a firm major program by the end of their sophomore year. It might very well be classics, with the realization that to get a job with a degree in classics, you'll have to go on for the Ph.D. and hope the subject is still being taught by the time you graduate. But you ought to have a firm program. That's why I say you should put serious thought into it and make a decision as soon as possible.

As it turned out, most students who took my advice to think seriously about their competing interests found that one of them did come forward. We all have many interests, but most of us—when forced—know where our strongest interest lies. I'm trying to force you.

Let's assume that you have chosen a major. Then you will have to—all college students have to—take required courses you don't like from teachers who aren't very good. The way to survive is to focus on the subject matter, not on the teacher. One hard lesson in this guide is that nothing anyone can possibly do will result in all your professors being good teachers. To reach your goal, you will simply have to put up with a few teachers who are not very good. I doubt that you will ever have a truly bad teacher. But you will have some that require accommodation and work on your part if you are to perceive them as at least minimally good. Your own minimal goal is to keep your professors from hindering your learning.

But what if the subject matter of a required course seems to have no relevance to your goals whatsoever? Required courses are determined by professors you are paying plenty because they know better than you do what is needed to reach the goal you have taken as your own. Or else, my daughter reminds me, they're senile old fools who haven't given the requirement list a thought since they compiled it fifty years ago. What can I say? You want to be a high school teacher? You take some courses in teaching methods, the value of which may not strike you immediately. Or, the old bugaboo, to get a degree in the humanities, you have to take a year of foreign language. A year doesn't begin to be enough to learn it, you'll never use it anyway, and so on. Right. Still, there are always good reasons for requiring courses that lots of students can't see the value of. I don't defend them all. I'm just telling you how to cope. Sometimes dumb subject matter is enhanced by a good teacher. But any subject matter can be presented badly. In general, almost any subject matter is interesting in itself, and my point here is that if you must take a course from a bad teacher or that has a dumb subject matter, the best way to get through is to force yourself to focus intensely on the subject matter.

Really learn it. Read the textbook. Read it again. Underline it and outline it. Read the supplementary readings. Take careful notes in class. Take detailed notes in class even if you don't understand what the teacher is saying, even if the teacher repeats what is in the textbook, especially if the teacher is disorganized. You will then learn at least one very valuable thing. That is how to pay attention and take notes in a difficult situation. That can be of use elsewhere. A year of foreign language might help you read and write better English, but one thing it is sure to do—if you concentrate on it—is teach you to learn a set of conventional rules and to work with a logical system (which is what a language is). Students sometimes seem to think that aptitudes for mathematics and foreign languages are in conflict, but in fact, they are alike in helping you learn to think systematically, about anything.

Learning to pay attention and document what is happening in a difficult situation is a skill of great use. Some of the most important things we have to pay attention to in life, after all, are neither clear nor very interesting. And one of the most important things you can learn is how to learn from anyone whatever the circumstances.

Concentrate on the subject matter.

Suppose your professor is mediocre. What I hope is that by concentrating strongly on subject matter, you will come up with questions that will draw the professor out. Help your professor to be a good teacher. You can get better teaching by being a better student. It's a challenge to pay attention in difficult situations. It's a challenge to learn to participate when you don't want to. It's a challenge to get something good out of a mediocre professor you cannot avoid because you are required to take this course to get your degree.

When I read complaints in student newspapers about bad teaching, my response almost always is: Nothing's perfect. Complaints about bad teaching are almost always made by good students who have had some excellent teachers. So they want all their teachers to be excellent, or even great. But, you know, all teachers aren't excellent, and very few are great. A lot of them aren't even entertaining. Most of them are pretty good, give and take a little. Whatever. But you can't, in your four years of college, avoid having some teachers who are *boring*.

"Boring! Boring! Boring!" as a student once replied when I asked her why she didn't speak up in class.

This reminds me of how Professor Richard Rudner once enlightened a persistent student who kept interrupting his lectures with stupid questions: "Shut up!" he explained.

Is a boring teacher a bad teacher? Not necessarily. Nor is an exciting teacher necessarily good. But if *you* find the subject matter exciting, and if you convey this to a teacher who seems to be pretty much of a loss, there is some chance that you might get an upgraded response. Anyway, don't get hung up on the teacher. What you're interested in is the subject matter.

But! But! But!

What if a professor actually does hinder your learning a subject matter? What if your teacher is truly bad? Suppose your teacher is one who says—and I've known this to happen—"Don't take this course, the subject is worthless, I was a fool ever to go into this field."

Complain to the dean. Don't go to your favorite professor to whom you can actually talk. Go to the dean. There are limits, after all.

3

College Teachers

And gladly wolde he lerne, and gladly teche.
—Geoffrey Chaucer, *Canterbury Tales*

Except for what used to be known as teachers colleges in which students are prepared and certified to teach in primary and secondary schools, few colleges and universities in the United States teach teaching. Members of boards of trustees and the administration think in terms of training scientists, scholars, engineers, administrators, people in business, medical doctors, and so on, but not teachers. This is particularly true for universities that do in fact produce virtually all college teachers. But there are almost no courses in college teaching—certainly very few that you could take for credit—and so there are very few college teachers who have had any formal training in teaching.

Many students are surprised by this. But it should not be surprising, because very few college and university professors chose their careers because they wanted to be teachers. Had they wanted to be teachers, they would have gone into primary or secondary education. Instead, the vast majority of your college professors did the work necessary to earn a Ph.D. because at some point in their schooling they fell in love with a subject matter. They wanted to learn more and more about biology, or English literature, or economics, or one of several dozen other subject matters. They wanted to spend their lives continuing to learn about these subjects, doing research, and discussing their work with other scholars in the field. Or, if that seems too starry-eyed, at least they wanted to be, say, working biologists, writers, or economists, but not necessarily teachers.

Oh, sure, they knew they would most likely get a job in a college or university, where they would have to teach. And some of them *are* natural teachers who love their subjects so much that even as undergraduate students they started teaching anyone who would listen. Your roommate who helped you get through a math course may be one of them. But my point is that being a teacher may not have been the primary goal of most of your professors.

The standard and thus easiest way to learn more and more about a subject matter and to join the world of higher learning and become an -ist or an -er is to enter a Ph.D. program. This is in fact about the only way to enter the higher level of the professions. The Ph.D. certifies that you are, for example, a biologist. The Ph.D. is not, however, a teaching certificate, and again, someone who has earned a Ph.D. has not necessarily had any training in teaching at all. This is very firmly indicated by the fact that someone who has earned a Ph.D. but not a teaching certificate is not permitted to teach in public primary and secondary schools. Someone who is qualified by the Ph.D. to be a college professor would have to take another year of teacher training to get a teaching certificate, which is why not many people with Ph.D.'s teach in primary and secondary schools, even if they want to.

Teaching certificates are not, however, required to teach in private primary and secondary schools. This shows that the requirement of certification for public-school teaching is partially a political matter. That is, a Ph.D. qualifies someone to teach in colleges and private primary and secondary schools without a teaching certificate. So why isn't it enough for teaching in public primary and secondary schools?

But why do we think a Ph.D. qualifies someone to teach in college? The Ph.D. is a research degree. A Ph.D. dissertation is a report on new or original research or scholarship in a field. It demonstrates the candidate's ability to do research—to learn—on the highest level on his or her own. Whoever holds a Ph.D. is certified to continue learning about a subject by doing research and producing scholarship. People with Ph.D.'s are supposed to contribute to the advancement of knowledge by writing and publishing so that the results of their work are available to anyone who is interested.

Note the very high moral tone here. The dissertation is supposed to be based on original research to provide new and significant knowledge in a field. The possessor of a Ph.D. has not only a license to work in a field but also a duty to further the advancement of knowledge in that field. It really is true that some of your professors feel that they have a calling, and they proselytize for work in their subject matter. Research is an exciting intellectual adventure, but you'll find that some of your professors are bored with it and spend their spare time perfecting their tennis game.

Although the Ph.D. is not a teaching degree, it is virtually impossible to get and keep a job as a college teacher without a Ph.D. At university colleges, this is because the administration employs certified researchers and scholars. At independent colleges, it is because only those who have earned a Ph.D. are conceived of as knowing enough about their subject matter to teach on a college level. The Ph.D. has thus become a requirement for being a college teacher.

The reason university trustees and administrators want the best *research* professors they can get is because the visibility of high-quality research and scholarship leads to the award of grants and contracts from government and industry and to contributions from private donors that may add up to as much or more money than the associated college takes in as tuition. The university operates mainly on the proceeds from its endowments and not from tuition. That is why at some universities the undergraduate college teaching program is the tail of a very rich, research-oriented dog.

But, then, who teaches in the independent colleges? As often as not, your professor in an independent college will be someone with a Ph.D. who could not get a job in a university. The higher the prestige of the university, the better the job. Better is defined here in terms of time to do research (that is, less teaching) and higher salaries. A professor's salary is a pretty good measure of how much teaching he or she does: the higher the salary, the less teaching. So if some professors at university colleges neglect their undergraduate teaching, some of those at independent colleges begrudge it because they had hoped to get a job in a university where they could do research and have time to write and publish.

But why can't professors at independent colleges do research, too? One reason is lack of facilities, but the main reason is that professors at independent colleges usually teach twice as many courses a semester as do professors at university colleges. If you do a good job teaching four courses a semester in a college, you simply do not have time to do very much research and writing. Contrast eight courses a year to one or two a year, which is the teaching load of some of the most prestigious professors in universities, particularly in the sciences. They also direct the Ph.D. dissertations of graduate students, sometimes quite a few of them, so they do more teaching than a one-course load suggests. But it is not teaching of undergraduates. In any event, the average load of a professor at a university college is two courses a semester; at an independent college, four courses a semester.

Thus to characterize the position of a university college professor as a teaching job is only half right. Of course it *is* a teaching job, but it is at least half a research job. And for university positions, candidates' teaching abilities are seldom considered in any but a cursory way. If a candidate's references say that he or she is an extremely bad teacher with no hope of improving, the candidate will certainly not be hired, *unless* those references also say that he or she is one of the best young researchers or scholars of this generation. If the candidate is seen as brilliant or has already published an important study, then that candidate will probably be hired whatever anyone says about his or her teaching, even at many independent colleges. Here is step number one in making a career in academe: Show promise as a researcher or a scholar by earning a Ph.D. and publishing your dissertation.

When new assistant professors arrive on campus, they have five years to prove themselves before the administration makes the decision (in the sixth year) whether or not to give them tenure. Tenure is a status of permanent employment that usually goes with promotion to the rank of associate professor. It is extremely valuable because whoever has tenure cannot be fired except for extremely gross dereliction of duty or criminal behavior. Very few professors are ever deprived of tenure once they get it. And very few who do not get tenure after the first five-year period can continue to find employment in colleges or universities.

What this means is obvious. The first five years of a professor's career constitutes the most important and difficult period of his or her life. If a professor doesn't make it during those first five years, he or she has probably lost the chance for a permanent job into which an enormous amount of preparation has been put. Four years in college and then four to eight years in graduate school earning the Ph.D., and now comes the crunch. Five years to publish enough to attain a reputation that will convince a committee of high-level professors and administrators that this assistant professor is hot stuff and will continue to produce. Only then will they give tenure. Only then will the young professor's career be secure. So here he or she is, twenty-five to thirty years old, possibly with a family, and there are just five years to *publish or perish*. It's no joke.

When I started teaching at a prestigious university, a distinguished older professor advised me to neglect my teaching. He didn't mean to goof off, he just meant that I'd better spend most of my time writing and publishing. The standard requirement for receiving tenure is that one publish a book or a series of articles that are innovative, seminal, or otherwise so important in a given field that the top people in that field have taken notice and will write letters of high praise for the candidate. The candidate must also demonstrate that he or she is still doing research. One does this by describing research that is under way, or by presenting a half-finished manuscript of a second book, or by having received grants or fellowships for further work. This is true even in many independent colleges not associated with universities.

What do you care about all this? You should care plenty. I am telling you who your professors are and what their concerns are. What I've just described is a situation that will help you understand two things. It explains why older professors who already have tenure are often more friendly and give you more time than younger professors who don't have tenure. It also explains why in every college in the land you will find extremely popular young professors being refused tenure. They simply have spent so much time being good teachers that they haven't managed to publish much, so they get axed. That is why you'll hear the macabre joke that if a professor doesn't yet have tenure, a teaching award is a kiss of death. As far as that goes, a tenured professor who wins a teaching award may not be the most likely candidate for promotion or for getting a good raise.

Sometimes it is not clear to new assistant professors that good teaching is not enough. I know of some who were told by college administrators that teaching was most important and that they did not have to worry about publishing. But when they came up for tenure with few or no publications, they got fired. The kindly senior professor who advised me to neglect my teaching was himself a superb teacher. And I had been hired in part because my references said I was a good teacher. But first things first: Get tenure.

I have never told new assistant professors to neglect their teaching, but I have lectured them along the lines that I'm now lecturing you. Anyone who intends to keep a job as a college teacher had better concentrate on research and publishing and not on teaching, at least until he or she gets tenure. Even after a professor has tenure, his or her raises and promotions are based on research and scholarly publication. Tenure usually includes promotion to associate professor, but if a newly tenured professor should stop publishing and give his or her all to teaching, then he or she will never be promoted to full professor, and his or her salary will remain low compared with the salaries of professors who publish a lot. Again, this is often as true in independent colleges as in university colleges.

Know your professors. The first thing you should know is that probably the majority of them did not choose teaching as a career. And if you are in a college at a university, you will find that very few of your professors consider teaching to be the primary or most important thing they do. Ask them what they are, and they'll say, for example, "I'm a geophysicist," and not, "I'm a teacher." And it is perfectly clear to everyone in academe—except, often, to students—that the faculty has not been trained to teach and is hired not primarily to teach but to do research and publish scholarly papers and books to advance knowledge and build their reputations, and thus enhance the prestige of the college or university.

Now *of course* these professors are hired *also* to teach. The courses *must* be taught. Colleges *are* designed to teach a lot of students. And in fact, there are plenty of professors who consider teaching to be the primary and most important thing they do. But perhaps you now understand why most of them don't concentrate on teaching at the beginning of their careers, and why some of them feel embarrassed or frustrated about preferring teaching to research later on. They are embarrassed because they were trained and hired on the basis of their promise as researchers and scholars, so to give that up as first priority is not to do their job. They are frustrated because professors who are top-rate researchers but poor teachers get paid a lot more than those who are top-rate teachers but poor researchers. And in independent colleges, some of your professors will certainly feel that they have failed to reach the goal of most Ph.D.'s, which is to get a job in a university where they can continue doing research and scholarship they began as graduate students.

The fact is that some college professors are pretty sour. Some professors even hate teaching. They find it a waste of time and students a bore. Because they don't want to be bothered, they may be bad teachers on purpose, in hopes that you will just go away and leave them to their research or brooding.

In fact, being a bad teacher is a lot of work, so they will usually not actually go out of their way to hinder your learning.

But suppose the professor you want to work with is a real bear. Sometimes the standoffishness of some professors is a defense against dabblers. You can dabble in college on an introductory level, but after you declare a major you are supposed to have serious interest. Professors get most frustrated at students in advanced courses who don't do any work. The way to show that you are seriously interested is to be persistent. Few professors will turn away anyone who truly wants to learn from them.

In fact, if you show yourself to be seriously interested in a subject, you are more likely to be recruited than rejected. A major goal of many professors on every college and university campus is to train young people to be co-workers with them. They really do change students' lives. If you want to be cynical, you can say they want cheap labor or free assistants. Tough. You have to pay for your education.

When I was in college, I just barely escaped becoming a Chaucer scholar, a pollen analyst, and a vertebrate paleontologist. My love affair with geology still continues even though I've been a professor of philosophy for thirty years. The professors who tried to lure me into their fields were mesmerizing. The good teachers are there if you want to do the work. More often than not, it is the student who holds back from making a life-committing commitment to a subject matter.

Let me tell you about one of those mad professors. Claude W. Hibbard was a professor of vertebrate paleontology at the University of Michigan. He worked not on dinosaurs but on tiny vertebrates, voles, shrews, creatures with bones so small that you had to sift for them by shaking dirt through fine screens at the excavations. Hibby was famous on his digs for getting students up and out to the site before sunrise so every bit of sunlight could be used. Often at dusk he would drive the pickup over and turn on the headlights so work could continue. He was just as driven in the laboratory, where there is an enormous amount of work to be done preparing the bones, analyzing them, drawing them, describing them, and writing them up for publication. You had to give your whole soul to work with Hibby. I was tempted but went on to other things. Hibby never suffered fools and never held his temper. And he worked all the time. At six one morning in his laboratory—he had been there since five—he was raging, perhaps at some student, and he dropped dead. He was in his sixties. Everyone was sad, of course, but no one could help smiling when hearing or telling about his death. That was the way for Hibby to go.

There seems to be no statistical evidence for it, but my experience is that professors who are really devoted to research in their fields are the best teachers, at least for students who know what they want and are willing to give their all to get it. These professors may seem impossible to work for because they demand so much, but they're still the best. These old bears, you give your all to them, and they'll be the great teachers you seek. And there are lots of professors like this, because most college professors are where they are because they fell in love with a subject matter. They think nothing else in the world is more important than learning about it.

4

Colleges and Universities

There was a man who was shown the buildings, the
offices, the classrooms, the libraries, the laboratories,
the president, the deans, the professors, and the
students, who then asked, "But where is the university?
I wanted to see the university."

—after Gilbert Ryle

Colleges and universities are founded by boards of trustees who either are self-appointed or are appointed by state legislatures or governors. A board of trustees consists of prominent
citizens who conceive of the purposes they or the legislators
want to accomplish. Then they raise money to build the buildings, hire the administration and faculty, and oversee operations. Boards of trustees continue to set the general purposes
of colleges and universities, and in particular, they continue to
raise money from both private and public sources. A few boards
keep close control even of details of teaching, while others
concentrate solely on raising money. Boards of trustees hire a
president who appoints a team of administrative deans. Other
than by setting the budget, trustees usually exert direct influ-
ence only when the administration displeases them.

The administrative staff, from the president to the lowest
assistant dean is ultimately answerable to the trustees, although
usually they interact directly only with the president. Thus for
private colleges and universities, it is not unfair to say that the
board itself employs the president to hire administrators who
in turn hire and supervise the faculty. The administration and
faculty of state colleges and universities are employed by the

state, and for them, state legislatures as well as boards of trustees have some say concerning the purposes and operations—and particularly the budgets—of these institutions.

Chairs or heads of departments straddle a fence in colleges and universities. On one side, they are part of the administration, but on the other side, they are part of the faculty from which they are almost always recruited. Thus chairs represent sometimes the viewpoint of the faculty and at other times the viewpoint of the administration. In either case, ideally they act for the good of their departments and students.

Deans are also often recruited from the faculty, but unlike chairs, they are not supposed to favor any specific department. They are fully a part of the administration, but they must be loyal *both* to the president and the board of trustees *and* to the faculty and students. Deans almost always strive to do what is best for the departments, faculty, and students, but sometimes the president or the board of trustees doesn't agree with the dean as to what is best. Also, a dean is always constrained within the limits of an assigned budget, portions of which are sometimes earmarked for specific purposes. A good dean is always negotiating and compromising to get the best outcome for the faculty and students.

The faculty is subordinate to the administration. I have said that the administration is employed by the board of trustees or the state to hire and supervise the faculty. In any other business—and whatever else they are, colleges are businesses—administrators would be seen as bosses and the faculty as workers, but the relationship is seldom described in these terms in academe. This is the result of more than snobbery, self-deception, and politeness. Historically, college and university faculties were self-administered, and some of this tradition remains. Faculty members thus have real power and in some cases can resist many of the intentions and orders of the administration and board of trustees. Often they can teach what and when they please, sometimes in defiance of the needs of the department or students and the demands of the chair and the dean.

The system, however, continues to evolve, and particularly in state colleges and universities, the employer-employee relationship is hardening, so that the administration (and not the faculty) sets goals and decides what is to be taught by whom. Decisions to abolish entire departments, for example, are made by administrators, not faculties. (One of the very few ways an administrator can fire a tenured professor is to abolish the job by eliminating the department.) But there still remain, particularly in private universities, departments and faculty members that have virtual autonomy.

Almost all colleges were originally founded for the purpose of teaching students. You might have thought this would be obvious, before you read this far. By now you know that if some universities were not founded for the purpose of promoting research and scholarship, boards of trustees and state legislatures have certainly since added research and scholarship to the original purpose of teaching. And at all major universities, research and scholarship have become primary.

For example, Iowa State College of Agriculture and Mechanic Arts was founded to teach the sons of Iowa to be agronomists, engineers, and veterinarians, and the daughters of Iowa to be home economics teachers and nurses. But it was also founded to promote research that would improve industry and agriculture in Iowa. And it worked, for, among other things, hybrid corn was developed there. The shift of priority to research over teaching is reflected in the change of name to Iowa State University.

An example of a private university in which the same shift has been made is Washington University in St. Louis. It was established to be "a great institution of higher education" for which teaching was clearly the primary purpose. Until the mid-1960s, it was a streetcar university, with 75 percent of the students coming from the city of St. Louis itself. But a conscious effort was made on the part of the board of trustees and the administration to turn it into a research university. Today 75 percent of the students are from out of state, and Washington University is conceived of and publicized as a research university.

What have these changes done to the teaching? I went to Iowa State College before the change and have friends teaching there now. And I started teaching at Washington University during the transition. I have to say that all evidence points to the fact that the teaching was pretty good before the change and has been just as good since the change. You can get a really good undergraduate education both at a big college in a state university and at a small college in a private university.

One of the great defenses of "publish or perish" policies and the stressing of research and scholarship over teaching is that professors doing original work in the fields are the best teachers. I've remarked that there is apparently no formal evidence that this is true. But there certainly is something to be said for finding professors who are actually doing the research and scholarship you are interested in learning to do yourself. Who better to show you the ropes than someone actually doing the work? Research professors are sometimes not good teachers in any conventional sense. You may learn from them more than by being an apprentice than by taking their classes. But this is part of the specialization of higher education, and during your junior and senior years, you'd do well to seek out the most distinguished professors in your department, whatever their teaching reputations.

For straightforward undergraduate teaching, it apparently doesn't make any difference whether your professors are active researchers or scholars or not. I've known some good teachers who don't even keep up in their fields. Of course this can be bad if the field is something advancing rapidly like biology, but it may not matter so much if the subject is Greek. The main thing shown by the fact that active researchers aren't in general any better (or any worse) teachers than professors who don't publish, is that the preference by universities for active researchers is not as such going to hurt the teaching. But of course stressing research does take away time and attention that professors might otherwise give to teaching.

What about graduate students as teachers? Some graduate students are a lot better teachers than your average professor. They know the system very well and can often help you pick courses and orient yourself. But graduate students are often so harassed and have so much work to do that they simply don't have time to put much effort into their teaching. Most of what I've said about professors as teachers goes for graduate students, too.

What about large lecture courses? You certainly will know of some famous professors in your college who hold the students spellbound. Everyone says you have to take the big lecture course from Professor Silvertongue, or your college education won't be complete. That may be true. But usually, the larger the audience, the lower the level the professor has to cast his comments. It is a law of nature that the content of lectures in large classes seeks the lowest denominator—not the lowest common denominator, the lowest denominator—of the students in the class. This is so the professor can satisfy everyone. But sometimes these courses are taught by great lecturers who can inspire students to take an interest in subjects they never heard of before. So try a few. And to get full value, sit in the front row and ask questions. Then despite the size of the class, the professor will recognize you. Overall, the rule is that the smaller the class, the better the teaching. This is because the smaller the class, the more individual attention you get from the professor.

Why *should* you go to college, by the way? I'll let my father tell you: "You know, when my father went to school you had to have an eighth-grade education to get a job selling vacuum cleaners door to door. And when I went to school, you had to have a high school diploma to get that job. But considering some of the college graduates I've seen applying for teaching jobs the last few years, I'm not sure today that I'd hire your average college graduate for a job as serious as that."

I don't know about selling vacuum cleaners, but I do know that today a bachelor's degree is about the lowest credential you can have if you want to be taken seriously in your application for any job above the level of working behind the counter at McDonald's.

You go to an undergraduate college to work for a bachelor's degree. The choice whether to go to an independent or university-affiliated college depends, as my father would say, on whether you want to be a big frog in a small pond or a small frog in a big pond. Universities can be very big ponds with tens of thousands of students. And as I've remarked, at universities graduate students often get the favored attention of the faculty.

In independent colleges, without graduate students, seniors often enjoy the status that graduate students do in universities. And at many independent colleges, you can work for honors, do research and fieldwork, and write a senior thesis that exhibits competence and training on the level of most master's theses at the few universities where they are still required. So at an independent college, you can sometimes get attention and training that you'd have to wait for until you entered graduate school, if you were at a university college. On the other hand, at a university college, if you're good enough, you can take graduate courses as a undergraduate. Your choices are often almost unlimited.

If you want to participate in lots of extracurricular activities—be a big frog—then the smaller colleges, either independent or university affiliated, are better than the enormous colleges associated with the huge state universities. If you want to participate in sports, and are good but not great, go to a college that doesn't give athletic scholarships. Of course at a big state university, there are many more activities, something for every interest, that might not be available at small independent colleges. In fact, I'm not so sure that the big-frog–small-frog analogy always holds. Big universities have a very large number of small ponds to be a big frog in.

The main problem at a university is that some professors get bored teaching introductory courses and give most of their attention to graduate students. You don't have that competition at a independent college, but you might meet professors there who don't keep up. Generally speaking, it balances out.

You can get a good education in almost any college. But there is one factor that does make a serious difference in your choice.

What do you intend to do after you get a bachelor's degree? If you do not intend to go on to graduate or professional school for an advanced degree, then it doesn't matter whether you go to an independent college or to a university college. But if you do intend to go on, it's usually better to go to a university-affiliated college, because some of your professors there will know professors in the graduate or professional school you want to apply to and can write personal letters of reference for you. At independent colleges, this is guaranteed to be true only at a few of the very best.

All in all, the quality of teaching you get is not going to depend specifically on whether you go to an independent college or to a university-based college. Except for one thing. You can get a good education wherever you go, but the quality of teaching is going to vary according to the basic ranking of the college. You're usually better off the better your college stands in national rankings of merit and prestige. At the lower-ranked state colleges, there is a problem compounded of overworked and frustrated professors on the one hand, and disinterested and not very good students on the other hand. If the general concern of the student body for education is low, and if there are large numbers of students who for whatever reason don't seem capable of or interested in applying themselves very well, then you won't get as good teaching there as you will somewhere where professors and students are enthusiastic. Surely I don't have to tell you this. Go to the best college you can afford and get into. You know which ones are best, and if you don't, there are plenty of guidebooks that will tell you.

OK, so go to a good college. But which one? It depends both on what you want to do during college and on what you want to do after you get your bachelor's degree. There is a pretense in the United States that we don't have sharply defined classes. This is not true. Graduates with the best educations from the best schools get the best jobs. If you want to get into the best medical school or the best law school, then you go to the best pre-med or pre-law colleges you can get into. Higher government positions are filled with people who have gone to Ivy League colleges. If you know what field you want to major in, then look in guidebooks to find out the best colleges for those fields. If you visit colleges to check them out, ask the professors in your fields of interest where they went to college, and where they think you'd get the best education in their fields. Don't be surprised to find that their advice may be to go to some other college than the one in which they are teaching.

5

Learning

Can you tell me, Socrates, whether virtue is acquired
by teaching or by practice; or if neither by teaching nor
practice, then whether it comes to man by nature, or in
what other way?

—Plato, *Meno*

Professors are trained, employed, tenured, promoted, and
salaried at the best colleges and universities—those that give
the most prestigious degrees—primarily on the basis of their
research and scholarly work. Most professors in all colleges
are trained to do research and not to teach, and they got their
Ph.D.'s at least as much because they wanted to do research
and scholarship, as because they wanted to be a teacher. Despite this, many of them do put their hearts and souls into teaching. And the vast majority of them are at least minimally good
teachers. The fact is, of course, that you want someone as
your professor who knows the subject matter well, and the Ph.D.
is a fair guarantee of that.

The first thing you should learn, then, is that you will
never see a majority of your professors rallying to make teaching of equal importance to research and scholarship in making
decisions about hiring, tenure, salary, and promotions. By now
you know why. It follows strictly from the fact that most of
your professors got their Ph.D.'s for love of a subject matter,
and because they want to be known as scientists and scholars
and to be rewarded for their research and scholarship. They
are teachers because colleges and universities are where the
laboratories and libraries are, or rather, because they can't make

a living just doing research, but they can get jobs in colleges and universities as researchers who teach or as teachers who do research. The most prestigious colleges are those whose professors have the most national and international visibility as a result of their research and scholarship. The colleges you most want to attend, those with reputations as "great institutions of learning," best fit the picture I am painting here.

So teaching is probably not the primary concern of the administration and faculty at your college. Never mind. That's the way it is. You don't want to live in a fantasy world, do you? And the system grinds out better teachers than you might have expected. Without requiring any courses at all in teaching, the system provides some of the best teaching there is. Of course it's also the only college teaching available. But if you don't like the teaching you get in college, consider the alternative.

On the one side there is teaching. On the other side is learning. I suggest that you can't do much about the teaching. That is, you have to learn to cope with it. But you can do a lot about the learning, because that's on your side. How do you learn?

Learning is a funny thing. Sometimes you think you've learned something, and then later, maybe years later, you're thinking about it and realize that you really never knew it, because you didn't truly understand it. But now you do. That is both a thrilling and a sobering experience. What if everything you think you know is like that?

That experience of sudden revelation and enlightenment shows you that learning has to happen in you. My father thought of teaching as coaching. Or coaxing. He could get kids to run faster, or to do more complicated algebra problems in their heads, than he could himself. But *they* had to do it themselves, and they had to work for it. It's impossible to put something into someone else's head. A good teacher presents something in such a way that it comes up in your mind in your own words and thoughts so that you can accept it or not, absorb it or not, depending on your own interests and abilities. But you can't just sit there and expect a teacher to pour knowledge into your brain.

So what *is* learning? Well, it happens when you pay attention and when you study, and sometimes it happens after you've studied a lot and relaxed. But you do have to study. Study is repetitive reinforcement. So how and where do you study? Where it is easy—in a quiet place where you won't be distracted. Alone or with others? Studying alone is one good way of forcing yourself to face up to and overcome your limitations. Some very good research shows, however, that students who study in small groups—I mean seriously working on something—do better in school than those who always study alone. What happens in these small groups is that you teach each other, and any teacher knows that the best way to learn something is to teach it. But being in a group can also be distracting, so I don't advise it for all your studying. In the end, you do have to know things on your own.

Speaking of distractions, let's talk about television.

Pat (my wife, who is also a college professor) and I have never owned a television set. This used to lead to some arguments with our daughter (name of Anna) when she was growing up. "Go to the Finkels if you want to watch television," I'd say, "they have a set." So she watched some television, but nothing like she would have had we had a set at home. The moral of this little object lesson is as follows: Soon after Anna went off to college she wrote home saying that we (her parents) were right. (Don't you love this story?) She was really amazed to find how many of her fellow students watched television four to six hours a day. "How do they get any studying done?" she asked.

First rule: Go cold turkey with television. Cut if off.

But you just watch the news programs? Read a newspaper every day instead. That doesn't, by any means, guarantee you a more objective presentation , but at least it forces you to read. And you get a lot more detail from reading than from television.

Here's the main trick of television. The scene changes so often because the shift catches your attention automatically, and you can't help but turn to watch what is going on. Just as you are getting bored—after ten seconds or so—the scene shifts again. You want to see what happens next. They've got you trapped. The only way to escape is to turn it off. I say nothing about the content of most television programs except that it is well below the level of intelligence of any college freshman I've ever known. If you want to be insulted by the television industry, what can I do about it other than rub your nose in it? No, the most destructive thing about television is how it chops subjects into such short time units, so that you are trained to pay attention to any one thing only for a few seconds or a few minutes at a time. You can't learn anything difficult this way. You begin to think that everything ought to be presented in short and easy bites. Nope, the world isn't that way. Everything on television may be simpleminded and easy to understand, but the world isn't. Cut out television and bear down on studying until you can work for hours at a time on one thing. The ability to concentrate is necessary for learning.

Now just as you have to figure out television to see why it is so bad for learning, you have to figure out your professors. Do research on them. Ask the department secretary if vitas and bibliographies of your professors are available. Look up their publications in the library. Read their books and articles. This is a good way to get to know what your professors are all about.

You also have to find out who the best teachers are. One way is to get the names of the best teachers in a field from someone majoring in it. You have to be careful, for the most popular professors are not necessarily the best teachers. There are limits about what you can do even if you discover the best teachers, obviously, for the best professor for you is usually the one teaching what you want to learn. This follows from the fact that the subject matter has to be basically more important to you than the teacher.

This brings us back to the professor who is a real bear,

but you have to take the course because it is required or because you have to know the subject matter. You have to work
harder in courses taught by such professors because the only
way to get their attention is to learn enough about the subject
that you can ask interesting questions. This means serious learning on your part. And it requires that you know what you want
to learn because it requires conviction to stick to it. It can be
very rewarding. But maybe it will be more work than it's worth?
That's possible, but you have to find out.

But what if you have to take a course from a professor
who is really off the wall? Suppose this professor's lectures
are trivial or disorganized or worse. There is still a way to
improve the situation, although it won't work for all professors. Give the professor written work. Write out in detail your
questions and speculations about the answers to them. Usually professors will respond to this. A similar move is to write
unrequired papers on the matters you are concerned to learn
about, then give them to the professor to comment on. This
doesn't always work because some professors are bad about
looking at papers, and some turn them back without making
comments on them. But it's worth a try.

What I'm suggesting is a lot of work? Yes, a lot of work.
To help, I offer you the old body builder's slogan—No Pain,
No Gain.

6

You

Know thyself.

—Socrates

My father was fond of saying to my brother, Jim, and me that if we really wanted to do some good as teachers, we should not have become college professors, but should have gone into primary-school teaching. He thought first grade, where kids learn reading, writing, and arithmetic (or used to), is most important. But sixth grade, he thought, is the greatest joy, because kids at that age are wild to learn, and a good teacher can help them learn almost anything. My father saw teaching as a calling. And that led to his disappointment at the end of his career in the late 1960s. Times were changing; educational standards were lowering; and he began to say that now all he was expected to do was keep kids off the street.

After he retired, he took a temporary job teaching history in a small college in North Carolina. He taught five sections of freshman world history.

"Now I understand," he wrote to my brother and me. "You guys are plumb lazy. I have to meet classes only fifteen hours a week, and all the rest of the time is my own. I sure made a mistake going into high-school teaching."

He was joking. He loved high-school teaching. And no wonder he thought fifteen hours a week was a snap. He already knew that subject cold and he didn't have to publish. He would have thought differently if, like most college professors, he had also been required to do research and writing.

You have the ability to learn a lot. Most of us never exert ourselves to full capacity. You are probably more limited by your goals than by your abilities. There is a connection between them, of course. Some people set goals obviously far beyond their abilities, even though they know that this guarantees failure. Others set such modest goals that they don't have to learn anything to reach them. Somewhere in between is a subject you can learn about and enjoy all your life. That's the subject I recommend to you.

The greatest hindrance to learning, however, is distraction. I've already raved about television. Here's another. There's a lot of talk these days about becoming a balanced person and living a full life. That's fine, but why be in a big hurry about it? College is a place a bit outside the ordinary world of business and commerce. Not much anymore, but still enough that you can spend long periods of time learning things that are not obviously useful right away. You can be one-sided for awhile. Enjoy learning while you can.

It used to be said that the purpose of going to college is to learn how to live the good life. Your professors today hope you will learn how to have a satisfactory life. There are many ways to have a satisfactory life, or to live a good life. But you can be sure that many of those who have become your teachers the way Plato's philosophers became kings (they had to be forced to leave their studies to rule the state as a matter of duty, not of desire) will recommend that learning to learn is the best way to ensure the enjoyment of life.

It is, you know, up to you.

Conclusion

An old rule about teaching is to tell them what you're going to tell them, tell it to them, and then tell them what you told them. The repetition probably helps anyone who listens all three times, but the point of the rule is that a professor hopes his or her students listen at least once.

Listen, my young friends, it is probably too late to change most of your teachers, but there is still some hope for you. If you are annoyed by the paternal, condescending tone of this admonition, so much the worse for you. Teaching is often very like teasing. A professor can turn students off by annoying them, but sometimes you have to annoy students to get them to learn. You know the old story about the Missouri mule? A man lends his mule to a neighbor who comes back and says he's got the mule hitched up but he won't go. So the mule's owner goes out to the field, picks up a two-by-four, and hits the mule right between the eyes as hard as he can. Then he says, "Gi-up," and the mule trots right off. "You see," the man instructs his neighbor, "first you have to get his attention."

I have described the system that produces your professors, and the circumstances—their interest in research and scholarship—that determine their self-images and survival in academe. Most of them don't set out primarily to be teachers. But then, you know, something happens to them that is fully in your favor. They take jobs as teachers, and whether they intended it or not, they become teachers. Most of them like teaching, and the majority do it well. Almost all of them are conscientious about their teaching. Some of them have even forgotten that they did not start out with teaching as their primary interest and goal in life. Those are the ones who will contest the picture of academe I present here. Some of them actually did start out with the primary goal of being teachers. It take all kinds.

It's a funny thing. No matter how distinguished for research or scholarship, the older a professor gets, the more likely he or she is to answer the question, "What do you do?" not as when younger with, "I'm an -ist" or "I'm an -er," but with, "I teach -y." As I said about your having to choose a subject matter, you become what you do.

Here is the bottom line. This system that concentrates on subject matter and the love of learning produces just as many good teachers as would one that concentrates on teaching and the love of teaching. You will have to work for it, but you can find a lot of good teaching in your college. Don't expect all your teachers to be first rate. There does not exist a profession of which all members are first rate. No institution composed of human beings is perfect.

The main lesson of this guide is: Don't be put off by the teacher or the teaching. Your professors may be perfunctory, obnoxious, or boring, but they *are* mostly on your side, and you *can* learn from them. But *you* have to figure out how, because all a professor can do is teach. You're the one who has to learn.

I'll conclude with the definition of a good student:

A good student is someone who has learned how to learn from anyone.

I want to give the last word to my sister, Connie. She went to college for a semester and then quit to get married. She had hoped to return to college after her four sons were raised, but it didn't work out that way. The old man always stuck my brother and me with the fact that Connie's IQ was twenty points higher than ours. Anyway, she works today in a semisupervisory job of the sort high school graduates can get. Every now and then, one of the part-time college students working with her lets off steam about how school isn't worth it, she's going to quit. Connie gets her aside, sits her down knee to knee, and looks her straight in the eye and says, "You want to end up at my age with a job like mine?"

Postscript

Suggested Reading

Postscript:
How to Change the System

If you really want to change the system, join it. Here's how: One hundred brilliant undergraduate students, four each in twenty-five different departments at your university get together. All of them graduate summa cum laude. All go to graduate school in twenty-five different departments at Harvard University. After they get their Ph.D.'s, they get jobs, one in each of the top one hundred universities in the USA. There they become hotshot teachers and researchers who publish a lot and get tenure early. They become chairs of departments, then deans, then university presidents at the top one hundred universities. *Then* they change the system. I am not joking. Revolution requires planning and lifelong commitment.

I suppose that's too naive. University presidents, like professors, are employees. It would be better for one thousand undergraduates to go to the Harvard Business School, get very rich, then one hundred groups of ten each get on the boards of trustees of the top one hundred universities. Clients (students) and employees (professors) can seldom change a system. Go where the power is.

OK. Time to get back to work. Read the assignment. Twice. Underline, make notes, outline. Study. Four years. Study!

Suggested Reading

Bok, Derek. "The Improvement of Teaching." *Teachers College Record* 93 (1991): 236–51. Bok thinks college teaching *can* be improved and tells how.

Clotfelder, Charles T. *Buying the Best: Cost Escalation in Elite Higher Education.* Princeton: Princeton University Press, 1996. Clotfelder gives some of the reasons, but by no means all of them, why tuition is so high not just in the Ivy League but also in the state universities.

Hexter, J. H. "Publish or Perish: A Defense." *Public Interest*, no. 17 (fall 1969): 60–77. A sustained argument that good researchers and good scholars are the best teachers.

Hilton, James. *Goodbye, Mr. Chips.* New York: William Morrow, 1934. A sentimental novel about a lovable old teacher.

Kolstoe, Oliver P. *College Professoring; or, Through Academia with Gun and Camera.* Carbondale: Southern Illinois University Press, 1975. Kolstoe tells it like it is with great verve and humor.

Livesey, Herbert. *The Professors: Who They Are, What They Do, What They Really Want, and What They Need.* New York: Charterhouse, 1975. There's a lot of good stuff here, but you have to make allowance for Livesey's indignation about professors really liking their jobs.

Meiland, Jack W. *College Thinking: How to Get the Best Out of College.* New York: New American Library, 1981. In this excellent book, Meiland tells you everything you want to know that I have not.

Readings, Bill. *The University in Ruins*. Cambridge: Harvard University Press, 1996. I really like horror story critiques like this one, but these ruins will continue to be inhabited for a long time.

Rosovsky, Henry. *The University: An Owner's Manual*. New York: W. W. Norton, 1990. Rosovsky was the dean of arts and sciences at Harvard University for eleven years. His title tells it all.

Sykes, Charles J. *ProfScam: Professors and the Demise of Higher Education*. New York: St. Martin's Press, 1988. Fun, but believe me, it's not that bad.

Watson, Richard A. *The Philosopher's Demise: Learning French*. Columbia: University of Missouri Press, 1995. The old professor goes back to school and bites the bullet.

———. *Writing Philosophy: A Professional Guide*. Carbondale: Southern Illinois University Press, 1992. A hard-core guide for getting tenure as a college professor, with instructions for writing papers, dissertations, and books in any field.

Richard A. Watson is a professor of philosophy at Washington University in St. Louis. He specializes in Descartes and Cartesianism. Besides the usual scholarly books, he has published a didactic trilogy: *The Philosopher's Diet: How to Lose Weight and Change the World*, *The Philosopher's Joke: Essays in Form and Content*, and *The Philosopher's Demise: Learning French*.

He has also published three novels: *Under Plowman's Floor*, *The Runner*, and *Niagara*.